THE SECRET POWER OF POSITIVE SELF-TALK

UNCOVERING YOUR INNER STRENGTH AND POTENTIAL

DR. JAGADEESH PILLAI

|| Dedicated to all wisdom seekers around the World ||

೮೨

Contents

Contents

Prayer

**"Om Bhadram Karnebhih Shrunuyaama
DevaahBhadram Pashyemaakshabhiryajatraah
SthirairangaistushtuvaamsastanoobhihVyashema
Devahitam YadaayuhSwasti Na Indro
VridhashravaahSwasti Nah Pooshaa
VishwavedaahSwasti Nastaarkshyo ArishtanemihSwasti
No Brihaspatir DadhaatuOm Shantih, Shantih, Shantih"**

The literal meaning of this mantra is: OM. O Gods! Let us
hear auspicious words from our ears. O reverent Gods! Let
us behold propitious visions from our eyes, let our organs
and body be stable, healthy, and strong. Let us do that
which is pleasing to the gods in the life span allotted to us.
May Indra, inscribed in the scriptures, bring us fortune!
May Pushan, the knower of the world, grant us prosperity!
May Trakshya, who vanquishes enemies, bestow us with
blessings! May Brihaspati bring us success!
OM Peace, Peace, Peace.

ABOUT THE AUTHOR

Dr. Jagadeesh Pillai is a renowned Guinness World Record holder, writer, and researcher hailing from Varanasi, also known as the abode of Lord Shiva. With a Ph.D. in Vedic Science and a range of creative ideas and achievements, he is a true polymath. He is the author of more than 100 books including Research Publications. Although his roots can be traced back to Kerala, the people of Varanasi hold him in high regard and affectionately consider him one of their own.

In 1998, Dr. Pillai was offered a job at Banaras Hindu University, but he left the position after only two months to pursue greater goals in life. He believed that in order to study Indian scriptures and engage in other creative endeavours, he needed to retire from the daily grind of working solely for money at a young age.

He started an export business from scratch, using the knowledge he had gained from a previous job in the industry. His intelligence and unique approach to business led to great success in a short period of time, earning him more in just a decade and a half than he would have in a lifetime working in a government job. Upon the passing of Dr. APJ Abdul Kalam, Dr. Pillai decided to leave the business and dedicate himself to reading, studying, researching, and experimenting.

During his tenure in the export business, Dr. Pillai traveled to over 16 countries, gaining valuable insight and experiencing the world and life in detail.

Dr. Pillai has achieved four Guinness World Records in the following subjects:

"Script to Screen" - In this record, Dr. Pillai produced and directed an animation film within the shortest time possible, breaking the previous record set by Canadians. He has also received numerous national and international awards and recognitions for this achievement.

Longest Line of Postcards - For this record, Dr. Pillai created a line of 16,300 postcards on the occasion of the 163rd anniversary of Indian Postal Day. The event also included a questionnaire about the Indian flag.

Largest Poster Awareness Campaign - Dr. Pillai designed an awareness campaign on the subject of "Beti Bachao - Beti Padhao" (Save the Girl Child - Educate the Girl Child) to achieve this record.

Largest Envelope - In tribute to the Indian Prime Minister's "Make in India" initiative, Dr. Pillai created a 4000 square meter envelope using waste paper to achieve this record.

Attempted - **70000 Candles on a 210 kg Cake** - To celebrate the 70th Indian Independence Day, Dr. Pillai attempted to light 70,000 candles on a 210 kg cake, which was recorded in World Records India.

Attempted - **Documentary on Dhamek Stupa of Sarnath in 17 Languages** - Dr. Pillai attempted to create a documentary on the Dhamek Stupa of Sarnath, dubbing it in 17 different languages. The result of this attempt is currently awaiting confirmation from the Guinness World Records.

Dr. Pillai is skilled in teaching the Bhagavad Gita, a Hindu scripture, and is popular among young people. He has helped many young people improve their lives through his motivational teachings.

In addition to teaching, he has composed and sung numerous Sanskrit Bhajans and patriotic songs.

He has also written and directed several short films and documentaries for awareness campaigns, and has volunteered with the police in both UP and Kerala to spread awareness about various issues through videos and photography.

Incredibly, he has produced and directed over 100 documentaries about the city of Varanasi, all on his own.

He has also helped and guided more than 25 boys and girls to achieve world records through creative and innovative methods. He is a multifaceted person who uses his intellect and the blessings given to him by God to excel in various areas. He is both a teacher and a student, always learning and teaching, and is able to master any subject he comes across.

He is a selfless social activist and motivational speaker who has overcome struggles and failures to become a successful and enthusiastic individual with a rich life experience.

In addition to his work with the Bhagavad Gita, he is also an efficient Tarot card reader, Astro-Vastu consultant, and a talented singer and composer. He has sung the entire Ram Charita Manas and Bhagavad Gita in his own compositions, and has sung the phrase "Lokah Samastha Sukhino Bhavantu" in 50 different languages. He is currently working on a detailed and scientific study of Vedas, Upanishads, Puranas, and the Bhagavad Gita. He has also composed and sung the Hanuman Chalisa and Gayatri Mantra in 108 and 1008 different compositions, respectively.

Awards - Four Times Guinness World Records, Winner of Mahatma Gandhi Vishwa Shanti Puraskar, Mahatma Gandhi Global Peace Ambassador, Kashi Ratna Award, Dr. APJ Abdul Kalam Motivational Person of the Year 2017, Mother Teresa Award, Indira Gandhi Priyadarshini Award, Bharat Vikas Ratna Award, Udyog Ratna Award, Vigyan Prasar Award, Poorvanchal Ratn Samman.

PREFACE

Do you ever catch yourself thinking negative thoughts about yourself? Do you struggle with low self-esteem and confidence? Do you find yourself procrastinating or struggling to stay motivated? If so, you're not alone. Many of us experience these kinds of thoughts and feelings at some point in our lives. But did you know that the way you talk to yourself can have a profound impact on your well-being and your ability to reach your full potential?

The power of positive self-talk has been long underestimated and overlooked, but it's finally getting the recognition it deserves. Research has shown that the words we say to ourselves can greatly influence our emotions, thoughts, and actions. Positive self-talk can help boost our confidence, increase our resilience, and even lead to better physical health. On the other hand, negative self-talk can hold us back and prevent us from reaching our goals.

In this book, "The Secret Power of Positive Self-Talk: Uncovering Your Inner Strength and Potential," we will explore the many benefits of positive self-talk and how it can help you tap into your inner strength and reach your full potential. You will learn practical techniques for identifying and overcoming negative self-talk, setting realistic goals, managing emotions and staying focused, using affirmations and visualization, building support systems, overcoming procrastination, and managing perfectionism. You will also discover the role of gratitude and mindfulness in positive self-talk, the importance of building self-esteem and confidence, finding your passions, adapting to change, and developing persistence and determination.

Through this book, you will gain a deeper understanding of how positive self-talk works and how to put it into practice in your daily life. You will learn to harness the power of positive self-talk to boost your confidence, increase your resilience, and unleash your inner strength and potential. Whether you're an entrepreneur, a student, a professional, or just someone looking to improve their well-being, this book is for you. So, join us on this journey to uncover the secret power of positive self-talk and unleash your potential.

1

Power of Positive Self-Talk and its Impact on Uncovering Your Potential

Have you ever talked to yourself? Of course, you have! We all engage in self-talk, whether we are aware of it or not. The problem is that much of our self-talk is negative and limiting. This negative self-talk can hold us back from reaching our full potential and achieving our goals. The good news is that we can change this negative self-talk into positive self-talk and unleash our inner strength and potential.

Positive self-talk is a powerful tool for personal growth and development. It involves speaking to yourself in a positive and supportive manner, instead of criticizing and berating yourself. Positive self-talk can help you build confidence, overcome obstacles, and achieve your goals. It can also improve your mental and physical well-being and help you lead a happier, more fulfilling life.

The impact of positive self-talk on uncovering your potential is profound. Positive self-talk helps you believe in yourself and your abilities. When you believe in yourself, you are more likely to take action and pursue your goals with confidence. Positive self-talk also helps you stay motivated and focused, even when you encounter setbacks and challenges.

Negative self-talk, on the other hand, can have a debilitating effect on your life. When you engage in negative self-talk, you are constantly criticizing yourself and telling yourself that you are not good enough. This can lead to feelings of low self-esteem, self-doubt, and a lack of confidence. Negative self-talk can also hold you back from pursuing your goals and reaching your full potential.

The key to unlocking the secret power of positive self-talk is to change the way you talk to yourself. This means becoming aware of your self-talk and making a conscious effort to change it from negative to positive. It takes time and practice, but with commitment and persistence, you can turn negative self-talk into a positive force in your life.

In this book, you will learn about the power of positive self-talk and how it can help you unlock your inner strength and potential. You will learn how to identify and overcome negative self-talk and develop positive self-talk habits. You will also discover practical strategies for integrating positive self-talk into your daily life, so you can start seeing the benefits right away.

Positive self-talk is a secret power that can help you unleash your potential and achieve your goals. It is a tool that you can use to boost your confidence, overcome obstacles, and lead a happier, more fulfilling life. By changing the way you talk to yourself, you can tap into this secret power and unleash your inner strength and potential. So, let's get started on this journey of discovery and unlock the secret power of positive self-talk!

"Positive self-talk is the fuel that propels us towards our goals and dreams."

౪

II

Identifying and Overcoming Negative Self-Talk

Negative self-talk can be a major obstacle to unlocking your potential and achieving your goals. It involves speaking to yourself in a critical and self-defeating manner, and it can hold you back from reaching your full potential. The first step in overcoming negative self-talk is to identify when you engage in it.

One of the most common forms of negative self-talk is self-criticism. This involves criticizing yourself for mistakes, failures, or shortcomings. For example, you might say to yourself, ***"I'm so stupid. I can never do anything right." or "I'm such a failure. I'll never be successful."*** This type of self-talk can damage your self-esteem and make you feel overwhelmed and discouraged.

Another common form of negative self-talk is perfectionism. Perfectionism involves setting impossibly high standards for yourself and feeling like you are never good enough. For example, you might say to yourself, *"I can never be happy until I achieve perfection." or "I need to be perfect in everything I do."* Perfectionism can lead to feelings of stress, anxiety, and self-doubt.

Fear-based self-talk is another common form of negative self-talk. This involves speaking to yourself in a fearful or worried manner about the future or what others think of you. For example, you might say to yourself, **"What if I fail?"** or **"What if they don't like me?"** This type of self-talk can hold you back from taking risks and pursuing your goals.

Now that you know what negative self-talk is and what it looks like, it's time to start overcoming it. Here are some strategies to help you get started:

Awareness: The first step in overcoming negative self-talk is to become aware of it. Start paying attention to the things you say to yourself, and make a note of when you engage in negative self-talk.

Challenge negative thoughts: Once you have identified negative self-talk, it's time to challenge it. Ask yourself if the thought is true and whether there is evidence to support it. If the thought is not true, replace it with a more positive and realistic thought.

Reframe negative thoughts: Another way to challenge negative self-talk is to reframe it. Instead of seeing a situation as a failure, for example, try to see it as a learning experience or an opportunity for growth.

Practice gratitude: Gratitude is a powerful tool for overcoming negative self-talk. By focusing on the things you are grateful for, you can shift your focus away from negative thoughts and towards positive ones.

Surround yourself with positive people: The people you surround yourself with can have a big impact on your self-talk. Try to spend time with positive, supportive people who encourage and uplift you.

Practice self-compassion: Finally, practice self-compassion. Speak to yourself with kindness and understanding, just as you would speak to a friend.

Overcoming negative self-talk is an important step in unlocking your potential and achieving your goals. By becoming aware of negative self-talk, challenging it, reframing it, practicing gratitude, surrounding yourself with positive people, and practicing self-compassion, you can turn negative self-talk into a positive force in your life.

"Words are powerful, and the words we speak to ourselves shape our reality."

୪୬

III

Uncovering Your Potential through Positive Self-Talk

Positive self-talk is a powerful tool that can help us unlock our full potential and live the life we desire. By speaking kindly and positively to ourselves, we can boost our self-esteem, increase our confidence, and overcome negative self-talk and limiting beliefs. In this book, we have explored various strategies for using positive self-talk to improve various aspects of our lives, from setting realistic goals and prioritizing self-care to managing emotions, building resilience, and finding and pursuing our passions.

It is important to remember that change does not happen overnight. The power of positive self-talk is something that takes time and practice to master, but the rewards are well worth it. By being persistent and determined, and by adapting and being flexible, you can find success and happiness.

One key aspect of positive self-talk is gratitude and mindfulness. Taking time to reflect on the things in your life that you are grateful for, and being mindful of your thoughts and emotions, can help you maintain a positive outlook and foster self-compassion. Additionally, building support systems and connecting with others can help provide a sense of community and encouragement as you work towards your goals.

Another important component of positive self-talk is overcoming perfectionism. Perfectionism can be a major roadblock to success and happiness, as it can cause us to feel overwhelmed and stressed. By learning to let go of perfectionism and embracing a growth mindset, you can tap into the power of positive self-talk to become your best self.

Positive self-talk is a transformative tool that can help us uncover our inner strength and potential. By focusing on the positive and speaking kindly to ourselves, we can build self-esteem, increase confidence, and achieve our goals. By practicing positive self-talk and incorporating it into our daily lives, we can cultivate a positive mindset and create a happier, more fulfilling life.

"The only limits we have are the ones we impose on ourselves through our thoughts and beliefs."

৪৩

IV

Setting Realistic Goals and Prioritizing Self-Care

When it comes to unlocking your potential and achieving your goals, setting realistic goals and prioritizing self-care are both critical components. Goals provide direction and focus, while self-care helps you to maintain the energy and motivation you need to reach those goals.

Setting Realistic Goals

Setting goals that are realistic and achievable is an important step in unlocking your potential. When your goals are too big or unrealistic, you may become discouraged and give up before you have a chance to reach them. Here are some tips for setting realistic goals:

Start small: Start by setting small, achievable goals that are easy to accomplish. As you build confidence and momentum, you can gradually set bigger and more challenging goals.

Be specific: Make sure your goals are specific and measurable. Instead of saying, "I want to be healthier," for example, say, "I want to exercise for 30 minutes every day."

Make a plan: Create a plan for how you will achieve your goals. This might involve breaking your goals down into smaller, more manageable steps.

Be flexible: Be willing to adjust your goals if they are not working for you. Sometimes, you need to try a different approach or make a change in order to reach your goals.

Prioritizing Self-Care

Self-care is the process of taking care of yourself physically, emotionally, and mentally. It is important for maintaining your overall well-being and for providing the energy and motivation you need to reach your goals. Here are some tips for prioritizing self-care:

Make time for self-care: Make time for self-care every day, even if it's just a few minutes. This might involve taking a walk, reading a book, or meditating.

Practice self-compassion: Treat yourself with kindness and understanding, and be gentle with yourself when things don't go as planned.

Take care of your physical health: Take care of your physical health by eating well, exercising regularly, and getting enough sleep.

Connect with others: Connecting with others is important for your emotional and mental well-being. Make time for friends and family, and seek support when you need it.

Find balance: Find balance in your life by setting boundaries and making time for the things that are important to you.

Setting realistic goals and prioritizing self-care are both essential for unlocking your potential and achieving your goals. By setting realistic goals, making a plan, and being flexible, you can stay focused and motivated. By prioritizing self-care, you can maintain your overall well-being and have the energy and motivation you need to reach your goals.

"Positive self-talk is the key to unlocking our full potential and living our best life."

છ

V

Building Resilience and Coping with Setbacks

Resilience and the ability to cope with setbacks are critical skills for unlocking your potential and achieving your goals. Life is full of challenges and obstacles, but with the right mindset and techniques, you can overcome them and emerge stronger.

Building Resilience

Resilience is the ability to bounce back from setbacks and challenges. Here are some tips for building resilience:

Practice gratitude: Focus on the positive things in your life and be thankful for what you have. This can help you maintain a positive outlook, even when things are tough.

Embrace change: Change is a natural part of life, and embracing it can help you to become more resilient. Try to view change as an opportunity for growth and development.

Focus on solutions: When faced with a challenge, focus on finding solutions rather than dwelling on the problem. This will help you to stay positive and motivated.

Seek support: Don't be afraid to reach out for help when you need it. Surround yourself with supportive people who can help you through tough times.

Learn from setbacks: Use setbacks as opportunities to learn and grow. Analyze what went wrong, and consider what you can do differently next time.

Coping with Setbacks

Despite our best efforts, setbacks are an inevitable part of life. The key is to learn how to cope with them and emerge stronger. Here are some tips for coping with setbacks:

Practice self-compassion: Be kind and understanding with yourself, and avoid negative self-talk. Remember that setbacks are a normal part of the journey.

Take a break: When you're feeling overwhelmed, take a break and give yourself time to recharge. This could involve taking a walk, meditating, or doing something you enjoy.

Seek support: Reach out to friends, family, or a support group when you need help. Talking to others can help you to gain a different perspective and feel more positive.

Stay positive: Try to maintain a positive outlook, even when things are tough. Remind yourself of your achievements and successes, and focus on what you can do to overcome the setback.

Learn from the experience: Use setbacks as opportunities to learn and grow. Analyze what went wrong, and consider what you can do differently next time.

Building resilience and coping with setbacks are both important for unlocking your potential and achieving your goals. By building resilience, you can bounce back from challenges and setbacks, and emerge stronger. By learning how to cope with setbacks, you can maintain a positive outlook and stay motivated, even when things are tough.

"Our thoughts become our reality, and positive self-talk can help us create a more positive and fulfilling life."

୫୭

VI

Managing Emotions and Staying Focused

Managing emotions and staying focused are essential skills for unlocking your potential and achieving your goals. Your emotions can have a significant impact on your ability to stay focused and motivated, so it's important to learn how to manage them effectively.

Managing Emotions

Emotions are a natural part of life, but it's important to learn how to manage them in a healthy way. Here are some tips for managing emotions:

Practice mindfulness: Mindfulness is the practice of paying attention to the present moment without judgment. Practicing mindfulness can help you to manage your emotions and reduce stress.

Exercise: Exercise is a great way to manage emotions and reduce stress. Whether it's a walk in the park or a workout at the gym, exercise can help you to clear your mind and feel more positive.

Connect with others: Connecting with friends, family, or a support group can help you to manage your emotions. Talking to others can help you to gain a different perspective and feel more positive.

Get plenty of rest: Getting enough rest is essential for managing emotions. When you're tired, it's easier to feel overwhelmed and stressed, so make sure you get plenty of rest.

Take breaks: Taking regular breaks can help you to manage your emotions and reduce stress. Whether it's taking a walk, meditating, or doing something you enjoy, taking breaks can help you to recharge.

Staying Focused

Staying focused is essential for unlocking your potential and achieving your goals. Here are some tips for staying focused:

Set goals: Setting goals can help you to stay focused and motivated. Make sure your goals are specific, measurable, achievable, relevant, and time-bound.

Prioritize: Prioritize your tasks and focus on the most

important ones first. This will help you to stay focused and make progress towards your goals.

Avoid distractions: Distractions can be a major barrier to staying focused. Turn off your phone, close your email, and eliminate other distractions to stay focused on your task.

Take breaks: Taking regular breaks can help you to stay focused. When you're feeling overwhelmed, take a break and give yourself time to recharge.

Practice self-reflection: Self-reflection is the practice of examining your thoughts and emotions. Regular self-reflection can help you to stay focused and identify areas for improvement.

Managing emotions and staying focused are both important skills for unlocking your potential and achieving your goals. By managing your emotions, you can reduce stress and maintain a positive outlook. By staying focused, you can make progress towards your goals and unlock your full potential.

"Words have the power to heal or hurt, and the words we say to ourselves can either lift us up or tear us down."

☙

VII

The Power of Positive Affirmations and Visualization

Positive affirmations and visualization are powerful tools for unlocking your inner strength and potential. Both techniques involve using the power of your mind to positively impact your thoughts, emotions, and actions.

Positive Affirmations

Positive affirmations are short, positive statements that you repeat to yourself regularly. They are designed to replace negative thoughts and beliefs with positive ones. Here's how to use positive affirmations:

Write them down: Write down your positive affirmations

and keep them in a place where you can see them regularly.

Repeat them regularly: Repeat your affirmations to yourself several times a day, especially when you're feeling low or when negative thoughts creep in.

Believe in them: Believe in your affirmations and trust that they will positively impact your life.

Personalize them: Personalize your affirmations so that they are relevant to your life and your goals.

Combine with visualization: Combine your affirmations with visualization for maximum impact.

Visualization

Visualization is the practice of creating mental images of your desired outcome. By visualizing your goals and desires, you can bring them closer to reality and unlock your inner strength and potential. Here's how to use visualization:

Get clear on your goals: Get clear on what you want to achieve and what your desired outcome is.

Visualize regularly: Visualize your desired outcome regularly, especially when you're feeling low or when negative thoughts creep in.

Make it vivid: Make your visualization vivid and use all of your senses to create a realistic image in your mind.

Believe in it: Believe that your visualization will come true and trust in the power of your mind.

Combine with affirmations: Combine your visualization with affirmations for maximum impact.

Positive affirmations and visualization are powerful tools for unlocking your inner strength and potential. By using them regularly, you can replace negative thoughts and beliefs with positive ones, and bring your goals and desires closer to reality. Start using positive affirmations and visualization today, and unlock your full potential.

"Positive self-talk is like a mirror, reflecting back to us the strengths and qualities that we possess."

☙

VIII

Building Support Systems and Connecting with Others

Having a strong support system and connecting with others is crucial to unlocking your inner strength and potential. It's important to surround yourself with positive, supportive people who encourage and inspire you to be your best self. Building strong relationships with others can provide you with emotional and mental support, help you overcome challenges, and provide you with a sense of belonging and purpose.

Building a Support System

Building a support system involves surrounding yourself with positive, supportive people who are there for you when you need them. Here's how to build a strong support system:

Surround yourself with positive people: Surround yourself with people who are positive, supportive, and encourage you to be your best self.

Connect with others: Connect with others who share your interests, goals, and values. Building relationships with people who are like-minded can provide you with a sense of belonging and support.

Reach out for help: Don't be afraid to reach out for help when you need it. Whether it's a friend, family member, or professional, asking for help can provide you with the support you need to overcome challenges.

Volunteer: Volunteering in your community can provide you with a sense of purpose and help you connect with others who share your values and interests.

Practice gratitude: Practicing gratitude and expressing appreciation for the positive people in your life can strengthen your relationships and build a strong support system.

Connecting with Others

Connecting with others involves building meaningful relationships and creating connections with people who share your interests, goals, and values. Here's how to connect with others:

Be genuine: Be yourself and be genuine when connecting with others. People are more likely to connect with you when you are authentic and honest.

Show interest in others: Show interest in others and listen to what they have to say. Building connections with others requires active listening and being present in the moment.

Share your thoughts and feelings: Sharing your thoughts and feelings with others can help build deeper connections and provide you with emotional support.

Join groups and clubs: Joining groups and clubs that align with your interests and goals can provide you with a sense of belonging and help you connect with others.

Volunteer: Volunteering in your community can provide you with a sense of purpose and help you connect with others who share your values and interests.

Building a strong support system and connecting with others is crucial to unlocking your inner strength and potential. By surrounding yourself with positive, supportive people and building meaningful relationships, you can provide yourself with the emotional and mental support you need to overcome challenges and achieve your goals. Start building your support system and connecting with others today, and unlock your full potential.

"The words we use to describe ourselves have the power to shape our identity and future."

൭ൠ

IX

Overcoming Procrastination and Staying Motivated

Procrastination can be a major obstacle to unlocking your inner strength and potential. When you put things off, you limit your ability to achieve your goals and reach your full potential. But with the right tools and techniques, you can overcome procrastination and stay motivated to reach your full potential.

Understanding Procrastination

Procrastination is a habit that involves putting things off until later. While it may seem harmless, procrastination can have a negative impact on your life by limiting your ability to achieve your goals and reach your full potential.

There are many reasons why people procrastinate, including:

Fear of failure: Fear of failure can lead people to put things off, as they may be afraid of not being able to do something well.

Perfectionism: Perfectionism can lead people to procrastinate, as they may be afraid of not being able to do something perfectly.

Lack of motivation: Lack of motivation can lead people to put things off, as they may not see the point in doing something.

Distractions: Distractions, such as social media, can lead people to put things off, as they may be more focused on other things.

Overwhelm: Overwhelm can lead people to procrastinate, as they may not know where to start or how to tackle a task.

Overcoming Procrastination

To overcome procrastination and stay motivated, you need to address the underlying causes of procrastination and adopt new habits and behaviors that support your goals and values. Here's how:

Break tasks into smaller parts: Breaking tasks into smaller parts can make them seem less overwhelming and help you get started.

Prioritize tasks: Prioritizing tasks and focusing on the most important ones can help you stay motivated and avoid procrastination.

Eliminate distractions: Eliminating distractions, such as social media, can help you stay focused and avoid procrastination.

Set achievable goals: Setting achievable goals can help you stay motivated and avoid procrastination, as you will be able to see the progress you are making.

Use positive self-talk: Using positive self-talk can help you overcome the fear of failure and stay motivated to achieve your goals.

Staying Motivated

Staying motivated requires a positive attitude and a commitment to your goals. Here's how to stay motivated:

Celebrate your successes: Celebrating your successes, no matter how small they may be, can help you stay motivated and focused on your goals.

Focus on progress: Focusing on the progress you are making, rather than the end goal, can help you stay motivated and avoid feeling overwhelmed.

Surround yourself with positive people: Surrounding yourself with positive, supportive people can help you stay motivated and avoid procrastination.

Use positive affirmations: Using positive affirmations can help you stay motivated and focused on your goals, even when things get tough.

Overcoming procrastination and staying motivated is essential to unlocking your inner strength and potential. By addressing the underlying causes of procrastination, adopting new habits and behaviors, and focusing on your goals and values, you can overcome procrastination and reach your full potential. Start overcoming procrastination and staying motivated today, and unlock your full potential.

"When we change our self-talk, we change our world."

೮౩

X

Understanding and Managing Perfectionism

Perfectionism can be a double-edged sword. On the one hand, striving for excellence and setting high standards for ourselves can be a positive and motivating force. On the other hand, when perfectionism becomes excessive and all-consuming, it can lead to feelings of inadequacy, anxiety, and stress. Perfectionism can prevent us from taking risks, trying new things, and engaging in self-care, all of which are critical for uncovering our potential and inner strength.

To understand perfectionism, it's helpful to recognize the difference between healthy and unhealthy perfectionism. Healthy perfectionism is a positive and adaptive form of perfectionism that involves setting high standards for oneself but also accepting that mistakes and failures are part of the learning and growth process. Unhealthy perfectionism, on the other hand, is marked by an unrelenting and rigid focus on perfection that is often accompanied by feelings of anxiety, self-doubt, and fear of failure.

Perfectionism can stem from a variety of sources, including childhood experiences, cultural messages, and life events. It can also be perpetuated by negative self-talk and unrealistic expectations. The key to managing perfectionism is to recognize its impact on your life and to make a conscious effort to shift your focus from perfection to progress.

Here are some strategies for managing perfectionism and promoting a more positive and adaptive perspective:

Recognize perfectionism as a thought pattern: The first step in managing perfectionism is to recognize when you are engaging in perfectionistic thinking. Pay attention to your thoughts and identify any patterns of self-criticism, black-and-white thinking, and all-or-nothing thinking.

Reframe perfectionistic thinking: Once you have identified perfectionistic thoughts, make a conscious effort to reframe them in a more positive and realistic light. Focus on progress, not perfection, and remind yourself that mistakes and failures are an important part of the learning and growth process.

Set realistic goals: Instead of striving for perfection, set realistic goals that are aligned with your values and priorities. Focus on making progress in small steps, rather than trying to achieve perfection overnight.

Practice self-compassion: Perfectionism often stems from a lack of self-compassion and a critical inner voice. Practice being kind and compassionate with yourself, and remind yourself that everyone makes mistakes and that it's okay to be imperfect.

Seek support from others: Building a supportive network of friends and family can help counteract the negative impact of perfectionism. Reach out to those you trust and seek their support, encouragement, and understanding.

Find healthy outlets for stress: Perfectionism can lead to high levels of stress and anxiety. Find healthy outlets for stress, such as exercise, meditation, or creative expression, and make a conscious effort to prioritize self-care and relaxation.

Be open to feedback: Seek feedback from others and be open to constructive criticism. This can help you see yourself and your work in a more objective and realistic light, and can also help you identify areas for growth and improvement.

Perfectionism can be a major obstacle to uncovering your inner strength and potential. By recognizing perfectionism as a thought pattern and making a conscious effort to shift your focus from perfection to progress, you can build resilience, reduce stress and anxiety, and unleash your full potential. Remember, the goal is not to be perfect, but to make progress, learn, grow, and live a fulfilling life.

"Positive self-talk helps us cultivate resilience and cope with challenges, setbacks, and failures."

౭౩

XI

The Role of Gratitude and Mindfulness in Positive Self-Talk

Gratitude and mindfulness are two important practices that can greatly enhance the power of positive self-talk. These practices not only help us to focus on the present moment and cultivate a positive outlook, but they also play a critical role in reinforcing positive self-talk and promoting resilience in the face of life's challenges.

Gratitude

Gratitude is the practice of recognizing and appreciating the good things in our lives. This can include the people, experiences, and possessions that bring us joy, comfort, and fulfillment. Gratitude helps us to focus on what we have, rather than what we don't have, and shifts our focus away from negative self-talk. Research has shown that practicing gratitude can have a profound impact on our mental and emotional well-being, leading to increased happiness, reduced stress, and improved relationships.

To cultivate gratitude, start by keeping a gratitude journal. Each day, write down three to five things you are grateful for. This could be something as simple as a sunny day or a warm meal, or as complex as a loving relationship or a sense of purpose in life. By focusing on what we are grateful for, we train our minds to see the positive in our lives and counteract negative self-talk.

Another effective way to practice gratitude is to express it to others. When we express gratitude to others, we reinforce our positive feelings and help to build stronger connections with those around us. Write a letter or send a text message to someone you are grateful for, or simply thank someone in person for their kindness or support.

Mindfulness

Mindfulness is the practice of focusing on the present moment without judgment. It helps us to calm our minds, reduce stress, and increase awareness of our thoughts and emotions. When we practice mindfulness, we become more attuned to our inner voice, and better able to recognize and shift negative self-talk.

There are many ways to incorporate mindfulness into your daily routine, including meditation, yoga, and deep breathing exercises. Another effective way to practice mindfulness is to focus on the present moment during simple activities, such as eating or walking. Pay attention to the sensations, sights, and sounds around you, and let go of any distractions or worries.

Mindfulness and gratitude also go hand-in-hand, as they both help us to focus on the present moment and cultivate positive thoughts and emotions. Take time each day to reflect on what you are grateful for, and bring mindfulness to your gratitude practice by focusing fully on your feelings of appreciation and joy.

The practices of gratitude and mindfulness are powerful tools that can enhance the power of positive self-talk. By shifting our focus away from negative self-talk and towards positive thoughts and emotions, we can cultivate resilience, improve our mental and emotional well-being, and unlock our inner strength and potential.

"The power of positive self-talk lies in its ability to help us find and pursue our passions and dreams."

৪৩

XII

Building Self-Esteem and Confidence

Self-esteem and confidence play a crucial role in our lives. They impact how we view ourselves and the world around us, and they can have a significant impact on our success and happiness. This chapter will explore the relationship between positive self-talk and building self-esteem and confidence.

What is Self-Esteem?

Self-esteem refers to the way we see and value ourselves. It encompasses our beliefs and feelings about our worth, abilities, and competencies. People with high self-esteem tend to have a positive view of themselves and their abilities, while those with low self-esteem may have a negative view and may doubt their abilities.

What is Confidence?

Confidence is the belief in our own abilities and the trust we have in ourselves to perform well in a given situation. It allows us to take risks, face challenges, and overcome obstacles. People who are confident are more likely to try new things, take on new challenges, and persevere when faced with setbacks.

The Connection between Positive Self-Talk and Self-Esteem and Confidence Positive self-talk plays a critical role in building self-esteem and confidence. When we engage in positive self-talk, we are more likely to see ourselves in a positive light, which can increase our confidence and sense of worth. On the other hand, negative self-talk can have the opposite effect, causing us to feel insecure and doubt our abilities.

Ways to Build Self-Esteem and Confidence through Positive Self-Talk

Focus on your strengths and accomplishments Take a moment to reflect on your strengths, abilities, and accomplishments. Write them down and read them often. Reminding yourself of what you are good at and what you have achieved can help to boost your self-esteem and confidence.

Challenge negative self-talk

Whenever you catch yourself engaging in negative self-talk, challenge it by reframing it in a positive light. For example, if you are saying to yourself, "I can't do this," try changing it to, "I may not know how to do this yet, but I am capable of learning and improving."

Use positive affirmations

Positive affirmations are statements that are designed to boost your self-esteem and confidence. Write down affirmations that resonate with you, such as "I am worthy," "I am capable," or "I am enough," and repeat them to yourself throughout the day.

Visualize success

Visualization is a powerful tool for building self-esteem and confidence. Close your eyes and imagine yourself in a situation where you feel confident and successful. See yourself performing well and feeling proud of your achievements. Repeat this visualization often to reinforce your beliefs in your abilities.

Surround yourself with supportive people

Surrounding yourself with people who believe in you and support you can have a positive impact on your self-esteem and confidence. Seek out friends and family who encourage and motivate you and avoid those who bring you down.

Building self-esteem and confidence is essential to unlocking your inner strength and potential. Positive self-talk can play a critical role in this process by helping you to see yourself in a positive light and increasing your confidence in your abilities. Remember to focus on your strengths and accomplishments, challenge negative self-talk, use positive affirmations, visualize success, and surround yourself with supportive people. With these tools, you can build self-esteem and confidence, unlocking your full potential and leading a fulfilling life.

"Positive self-talk helps us build self-esteem, confidence, and a growth mindset."

೮౩

XIII

Finding and Pursuing Your Passions

In this chapter, we will explore the importance of finding and pursuing your passions and how positive self-talk can play a significant role in helping you discover and achieve your goals and aspirations.

Discovering your passions is an essential part of personal growth and fulfillment. It is a journey of self-discovery that helps you understand what truly makes you happy and what you are passionate about. When you identify your passions, you are able to focus your time, energy, and resources on things that bring you joy and fulfillment. This, in turn, enhances your overall well-being and happiness.

However, discovering your passions is not always a straightforward process. Many people struggle to identify what they are truly passionate about, and they may feel overwhelmed by the choices available to them. This is where positive self-talk comes in. By practicing positive self-talk, you can overcome self-doubt, anxiety, and negativity, and become more confident and self-assured in your pursuit of your passions.

Positive self-talk can also help you stay motivated and focused as you work towards your goals. It can give you the courage and determination to take risks and overcome obstacles, and help you maintain a positive outlook and attitude, even in the face of adversity.

There are several strategies you can use to find and pursue your passions:

Identify your values and interests.

Start by identifying what you value most in life and what you enjoy doing in your free time. What are the things that make you feel fulfilled and happy? What activities or hobbies do you enjoy that you could see yourself doing for the rest of your life?

Explore new experiences.

Try new things, and keep an open mind. Take up a new hobby, join a club, or travel to new places. By exposing yourself to new experiences, you can broaden your horizons and discover new passions and interests.

Get feedback from others.

Seek the opinions of your friends, family, and colleagues. Ask them what they think you are good at and what they think you enjoy doing. This can provide valuable insights and help you gain a better understanding of your strengths and passions.

Take small steps.

Don't be afraid to start small and take baby steps towards your goals. Every little bit counts, and you will be surprised at how quickly you can make progress when you stay focused and positive.

Surround yourself with supportive people.

Surround yourself with people who share your passions and support your goals. They can provide you with the encouragement, motivation, and inspiration you need to pursue your passions with confidence and determination.

Finding and pursuing your passions is an essential part of personal growth and fulfillment. Positive self-talk can play a significant role in helping you overcome self-doubt, anxiety, and negativity, and become more confident and self-assured in your pursuit of your passions. By using the strategies outlined in this chapter, you can take the first steps towards discovering and achieving your goals and aspirations, and unlock your full potential.

"The words we use to talk to ourselves set the tone for our lives, and positive self-talk can bring joy, happiness, and success."

છ

XIV

Learning to Adapt and Be Flexible

One of the key components of positive self-talk and unlocking your full potential is the ability to be flexible and adapt to changes and challenges in life. In a world that is constantly evolving, it is crucial to have the ability to adjust to new circumstances and continue to grow and thrive. In this chapter, we will explore the importance of adaptability and flexibility in developing a positive self-talk mindset, and how it can help you to overcome obstacles and reach your goals.

Why is adaptability important?

Adaptability is a crucial life skill because it allows you to navigate through changes and challenges in a positive and productive way. When you are adaptable, you are better equipped to handle unexpected situations and changes in your life, which can often be stressful and overwhelming.

Being adaptable also means that you are open-minded and willing to try new things, which can lead to personal growth and new experiences.

How can you develop adaptability?

Developing adaptability starts with having a growth mindset and being open to change. This means being willing to learn and try new things, and recognizing that making mistakes is part of the learning process. Additionally, practicing mindfulness and being present in the moment can help you to be more adaptable, as it allows you to stay calm and focused in stressful situations.

Another way to develop adaptability is to be proactive in seeking out new experiences and challenges. This can involve taking on new responsibilities at work, trying new hobbies, or traveling to new places. These experiences can help you to develop new skills, build confidence, and become more comfortable with change and uncertainty.

The role of positive self-talk in adaptability

Positive self-talk plays a critical role in helping you to be more adaptable and flexible in your life. When you engage in positive self-talk, you are reinforcing a growth mindset and a positive outlook, which can help you to approach challenges with confidence and resilience. Additionally, positive self-talk can help to reduce stress and anxiety in challenging situations, allowing you to stay calm and focused, and make better decisions.

Examples of positive self-talk for adaptability

"I am capable of handling change and adapting to new situations."

"I am open to learning and trying new things."

"I am resilient and can overcome any challenges that come my way."

"I embrace change and see it as an opportunity for growth and learning."

Adaptability and flexibility are essential components of a positive self-talk mindset and unlocking your full potential. By developing a growth mindset, seeking out new experiences, and engaging in positive self-talk, you can cultivate the ability to handle change and challenges with confidence and resilience. Remember, change is a constant in life, and being adaptable is key to reaching your goals and living a fulfilling life.

"Positive self-talk is not just a tool for personal growth, it's a key to unlocking our full potential and living our best life."

৩

XV

The Power of Persistence and Determination

One of the most important factors in uncovering your inner strength and potential is persistence and determination. When you are faced with challenges or obstacles, it can be easy to give up and abandon your goals. However, those who possess a strong sense of determination and persistence are much more likely to achieve success and reach their full potential.

Persistence is the act of continuing to work towards your goals, even when faced with setbacks or obstacles. It involves a strong commitment to success, even in the face of adversity. Determination is the drive and willpower to see things through, no matter what. Together, persistence and determination provide a powerful combination that can help you overcome obstacles, achieve your goals, and uncover your inner strength and potential.

The benefits of persistence and determination are many. By remaining focused on your goals, you can maintain a positive attitude and a sense of purpose, even in the face of adversity. This can help you avoid becoming discouraged or disheartened, and can keep you motivated to continue working towards your goals. Additionally, by persevering, even in the face of difficulties, you can develop a sense of pride and accomplishment, which can boost your self-esteem and confidence.

Another benefit of persistence and determination is that they can help you develop resilience. Resilience is the ability to bounce back from setbacks, challenges, and obstacles. By continuing to work towards your goals, even in the face of adversity, you can build your resilience, which can help you cope better with stress and challenges in the future.

However, persistence and determination can be challenging to develop and maintain. Here are some tips to help you build persistence and determination in your own life:

Set clear and achievable goals: By setting clear, measurable, and achievable goals, you can maintain focus and direction, and avoid becoming discouraged or disheartened.

Focus on progress, not perfection: Instead of focusing on perfection, focus on making progress towards your goals. Celebrate your achievements, no matter how small, and use them as motivation to continue working towards your goals.

Surround yourself with supportive people: Surround yourself with people who believe in you and your goals. Having a supportive network can help you stay motivated, and can provide you with encouragement and support when you need it most.

Stay positive and optimistic: A positive attitude and optimistic outlook can help you overcome challenges and setbacks, and can keep you motivated to continue working towards your goals.

Learn from failures: When faced with setbacks or failures, use them as opportunities to learn and grow. Reflect on what went wrong and use this knowledge to inform your future efforts.

Persistence and determination are powerful tools for uncovering your inner strength and potential. By focusing on your goals, maintaining a positive attitude, and persevering, even in the face of adversity, you can achieve success and reach your full potential. Remember, success is not about perfection, but about progress. Keep working towards your goals, and with time, determination, and persistence, you can achieve anything you set your mind to.

"Positive self-talk is the voice of our inner strength and potential, guiding us towards a brighter future."

৪০

OTHER BOOKS OF THE AUTHOR

1. The Moments When I Met God
2. Kashiyile Theertha Pathangal
3. Guru Gyan Vani
4. Abhiprerak Gita
5. Assi Se Jain Ghat Tak
6. Hopelessness Of Arjuna
7. The Soul And It's True Nature
8. Sense Of Action (Karma)
9. Action Through Wisdom
10. Action Through Wisdom
11. Theory And Practical Of Every Action
12. Logical Understanding Of The Supreme
13. The Imperishable Supreme
14. Yatra Nishadraj Se Hanuman Ghat Tak
15. Yatra Karnatak Ghat Se Raja Ghat Tak
16. Yatra Pandey Ghat Se Prayagraj Ghat Tak
17. Yatra Ranjendra Prasad Ghat Se Dattatreya Ghat Tak
18. Yaatrasindhiya Ghat Se Gwaliar Ghat Tak
19. Yatra Mangala Gauri Ghat Se Hanuman Gadhi Ghat Tak
20. Yatra Gaay Ghat Se Nishad Ghat Tak
21. Maa Ganga, Ghaten Evm Utsav
22. Ganga Arti Dev Deepavali Evam Any Utsav
23. Potentials Of Digitalized India
24. Vedic Consciousness
25. A Brief Introduction To Vedic Science
26. Kashi Ke Barah Jyotirling
27. Impact Of Motivation
28. Let's Have A Milky Way Journey
29. Color Therapy In A Nutshell

30. Rigveda In A Nutshell
31. Yajurveda In A Nutshell
32. Samveda In A Nutshell
33. Atharva Veda In A Nutshell
34. Ayushman Bhava - Ayurveda
35. Srimad Bhagavad Gita And Upanishad Connection
36. Srimad Bhagavad Gita - An Attempt To Summarize Each Chapter.
37. Facts And Impact Of Nakshatra
38. Astro Gems - Navaratna
39. Ekadashi - A Concise Overview
40. A Concise View Of Hanuman Chalisa
41. Inspirational Gita
42. Nakshatraranyam
43. Summary Of 18 Mahapuranas
44. Synopsis Of 18 Upa Puranas
45. Rigvediya Upanishads
46. Shukla Yajurvediya Upanishads
47. Krishna Yajurvediya Upanishads
48. Samavediya Upanishads
49. Atharvavediya Upanishads
50. The Seven Great Sages
51. From Rocket Scientist To President Dr. Apj Abdul Kalam
52. The Visionary's Voice - Quotes Of Dr. Apj Abdul Kalam
53. The Wisdom Of Swami Vivekananda: Insights And Inspiration From A Legendary Spiritual Teacher
54. Ayurvedic Remedies From The Garden
55. Sages And Seers
56. Rising Strong – Motivational Stories Of Women
57. Beyond Flames -Mystery Stories Of Funeral Ghat Manikarnika
58. The Origins Of Tulsi: A Look At The Mythological Roots Of The Plant"

CONTACT

DR. JAGADEESH PILLAI

MBA & PhD in Vedic Science

Four Times Guinness World Record Holder

Winner of Mahatma Gandhi Vishwa Shanti Puraskar and Global Peace Ambassador

Gemology, Astro & Vastu Consultant - Spiritual Counselor

Consultant for designing World Record Ideas

Efficient Tarot Card Reader

9839093003

myrichindia@gmail.com

drjagadeeshpillai@facebook

drjagadeeshpillai@instagram
jagadeeshpillai@youtube

www. JAGADEESHPILLAI.com

෬

|| LOKAHA SAMASTHAHA SUKHINO BHAVANTU ||

ॐ

Printed by Libri Plureos GmbH in Hamburg, Germany